Face the Rain:
Mental Health Essentials

Photography / Written by
Arlen Rundvall © 2024

Also by Arlen Rundvall:

The Bipolar Guide to the Gift

Fracture: A Memoir
www.arlenrundvall.com

© Copyright 2024 *Arlen Rundvall*.

All rights reserved. No part of this publication may be reproduced, stored in a retrieval system, or transmitted, in any form or by any means, electronic, mechanical, photocopying, recording, or otherwise, without the written prior permission of the author.

Order this book online at www.trafford.com
or email orders@trafford.com

Most Trafford titles are also available at major online book retailers.

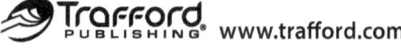 www.trafford.com
North America & international
toll-free: 844 688 6899 (USA & Canada)
fax: 812 355 4082

Our mission is to efficiently provide the world's finest, most comprehensive book publishing service, enabling every author to experience success. To find out how to publish your book, your way, and have it available worldwide, visit us online at www.trafford.com

Because of the dynamic nature of the Internet, any web addresses or links contained in this book may have changed since publication and may no longer be valid. The views expressed in this work are solely those of the author and do not necessarily reflect the views of the publisher, and the publisher hereby disclaims any responsibility for them.

Any people depicted in stock imagery provided by Getty Images are models, and such images are being used for illustrative purposes only.
Certain stock imagery © Getty Images.

ISBN: 978-1-6987-1689-3 (sc)
ISBN: 978-1-6987-1690-9 (e)

Print information available on the last page.

Trafford rev. 04/26/2024

Life experiences dealing with mental illness have taught me a few things the hard way. I have lived as a mental illness family member, worked as a Safety Advisor, and also personally faced mental illness. It can be a tough journey.

My wife, RosaLee prompted me to write these condensed essentials of living with mental illness. She has helped me to face the rain and to live for better days.

I hope that this helps you, and your loved ones out. Yes, you are worthy. You deserve good in your life.

Consult with your health professionals before taking any of this counsel.

This book is dedicated to you, the reader. May you find some comfort and encouragement in these pages.

Storms pass through the pain

Face the rain to brighter days

No words can describe what I feel inside

www.arlenrundvall.com

I was a family member of someone with mental illness before I experienced mental illness myself. Yet when I think about it thoroughly, perhaps I was always ill in some way. I always felt I was in my own world. I didn't want to interact with this world of grown ups. I wanted to continue to play as a kid. It felt like my timing was off.

I learned to speak in full sentences as a toddler and then I went somewhat mute. I developed a bit of my own language that my sister could understand. She was four years older than me.

One of my biggest memories from kindergarten is trying to speak and being teased by a boy from my sister's class. He made up a name for me and he mocked me. I believe this contributed to a fear of bringing attention to myself. From then on my goal in school was to blend in. At least that was my internal experience.

Soon after the mocking we discovered that it was my hearing that was causing issues and as it cleared up I was able to speak normally, if you can say such a thing. What is normal as we learn of all the flavours of human experience out there?

My early speaking challenge contributed to a social awkwardness that wasn't fully countered until my early twenties. I then experienced manic episodes that introduced me as a social extrovert, part time at least.

It is a shame that we describe a human experience as ill or well. Are we not still human and deserving to love and to be loved? Does not each aspect of the experience portray a piece of being human? Our health is one of the most important aspects of our human being existence.

I share with you a bit of my past to connect with you. You are not alone. We are each on a journey. My goal in this little book is to provide you with shortcut prompts that you can read and launch from to a better place. This is a book of encouragement.

When I was twenty, I was hospitalized for the first time for mental health reasons. I went into Detox and went cold turkey off of street drugs and then I fell deeper into a drug-induced-psychosis. I had to be protected from harming myself. I found the first psychiatric hospitalization to be an extremely jarring experience. It was brutal, and I was hard on myself.

Sometimes we can be so messed up that we need others to help us in these times of crises. A nurse gave me a book with a chapter on Abraham Lincoln and the troubles he faced when he was younger. He had to be protected from himself for a while. It really helped me to read a story of someone who was able to go on from suffering and to have a life of meaning.

You may be down and out right now. Try to focus on a brighter future. You can do it a small step at a time. Your present situation is not locked in. You can and will change to your better existence. Keep trying. You are worth it.

In developing a safety talk at work, I came across two important words that are seven letters long and start with "ch" and end with "ces." One you make and one you take. They are choices and chances. We have to learn to calculate the chances that we take and be empowered with the choices that we make.

So much is beyond our control. Learn to change what you can. We need to feel that we are in control of something and making some progress in some area of our lives. Even if it is something small, celebrate your empowerment.

Let go of what you cannot change. There is much going on in the world and plenty of media coverage covering it. If you find that it is too much, try reducing your consumption of the news and media. Concentrate on subjects that encourage you.

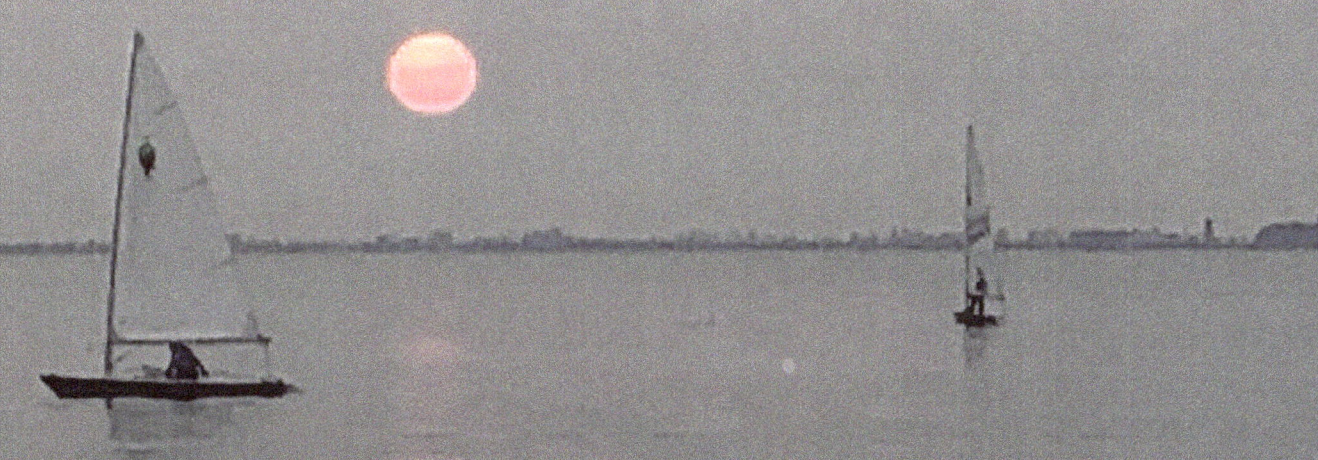

Sometimes slow and steady
Is really the best

www.arlenrundvall.com

We do better at times to have the focus outside of ourselves. If you want to be involved in changing a part of the world, go for it. But be careful when you help others. We can be taken down paths of obsession that can be hard on us. We can be inspired to give away all of our possessions for a good cause. Please strive to look after yourself, then you will be able to help others more. It is up to each of us to learn to be experts in our self-care so that we can give something to others in our lives.

Recognize that the brain is physical and that it can have physical things wrong with it. We need to look after the physical brain health. It is interesting that we accept physical illnesses more readily than mental illnesses. We all tend to face health challenges if we live long enough.

Brain health affects our minds and our lives with thinking, actions, impulses, and feelings. It can be complicated to develop control over thinking, actions, impulses and feelings. It can take time to gain this control. Start in small ways and give yourself a break.

Remember that we are physical beings that need to look after the basics of exercise, good nutrition and sleep. We are each different and have different needs. We still dwell in our physical bodies and need to use the physical to maximize our experience.

There have been times in my life when I have not been able to sleep much. I found one solution was to lie down with my feet slightly above the level of my heart and to lower my stimulation with low or no light. This can be challenging to do if you are wound up. It can take stages sometimes to slow down. Perhaps try listening to relaxing music.

I was preparing to speak once at a hotel conference room. I was scoping out the room before the event and talked to a person setting up chairs. My speaking subject was about bipolar and the person setting up chairs was bipolar. They said that they harnessed the energy by doing several physical jobs to remedy all the energy that they had at times. This is an interesting approach that has some value. I found it hard to pace myself and stay injury free. As we age it can be harder to utilize the body to harness the energies as well. I have needed to adapt my physical pursuits to be different as I have aged.

Learn to listen to your body and mind, and rest when needed. We have to develop the skill of pacing ourselves to avoid risking exhaustion or triggering our own crises. We have to learn to not wear out our bodies with our minds perhaps pushing relentlessly, and at other times we are lethargic and need to push ourselves. We need to learn to be our own coaches who take different approaches at different times to praise, nurture, and motivate.

Know what stimulates you to bring you down or up from where you are at. It can take time to develop the self-knowledge of how certain music, people, and activities affect you. We need to develop a self-awareness to be empowered. How does everything affect you?

It is paramount to know your stressors and healthy inlets. What helps you out? How can you process things effectively and develop healthy outlets? An outlet could be anything expending energy like playing guitar, crocheting, or going for a walk.

Learn to know where you are at in the moment so that you can recognize what you are going through. Some illnesses take us down a road that blurs our perspective. We need to clear the fog to see our true selves. This can take time and we need to pace ourselves to not progress too quickly.

Remind yourself to inhale through the nose and exhale slowly to bring yourself into the moment of where you are at. Involve your senses to get grounded in the here and now. We need to counter distractions to develop focus.

Make choices with the help of others to guide you, and learn to make your own decisions to anticipate and live with the consequences. We have the most to gain or lose from our choices and the chances that we take. We have to learn to empower ourselves to make the right choices. We need to learn to look ahead to embrace the consequences and anticipate how things will affect us.

Accept the present reality as it is and remember to breathe. Just like in a physical illness or injury, the pain can be worse at the start. When we first experience something it can be overwhelming and confusing. Others may further complicate our reality by not being supportive. We need to focus on who we truly are and on any positives that we may discover.

When you first face something, it tends to rate higher on the stress level. A medical professional is telling me that I have a mental illness, that my loved one has a mental illness. Get away! This is horrible. It can't be true. Denial would be one stage of facing something for the first time. Anger, despair, fear, self-loathing, and even relief could be part of your experiences in first grieving a diagnoses.

It can be challenging to get a proper diagnoses. It can take years. Mental illness can take a long time to even get to the point of involvement with a professional. We can be living less severe consequences of illness for a long time and we can get set in these ways and get stuck. Times of crises tend to bring us into more contact with mental health professionals.

Don't let your diagnoses limit or define you. Remember that you are a human being first and foremost that lives life before and after a diagnoses.

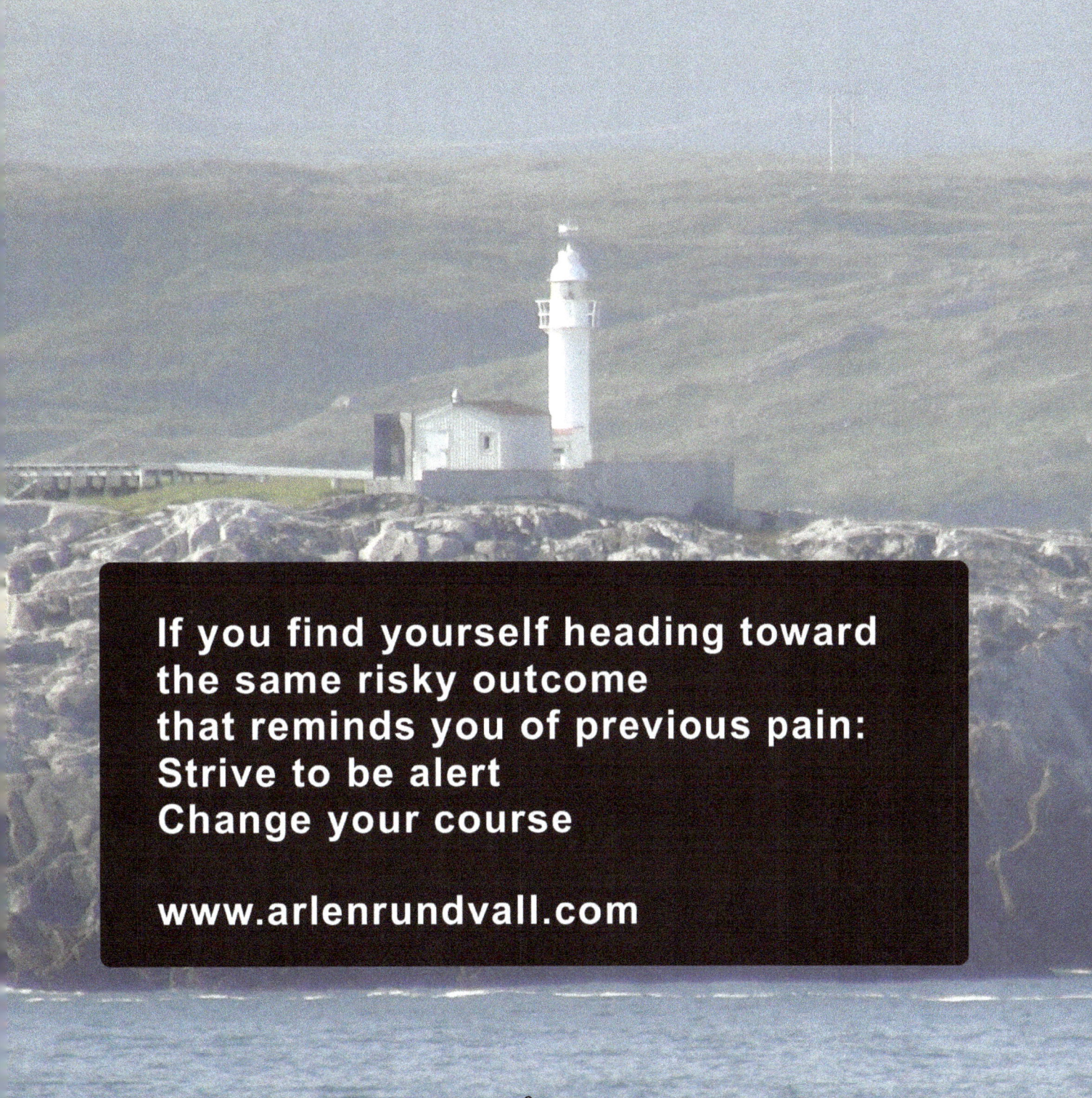

You are not the only one to experience your struggles. There are billions of people living right now and many of us experience similar obstacles. You are not alone. Reach out to others that are further down the path that you are on. Reach out to those struggling on the journey that used to be such a struggle for you. You have learned ways to face your challenges, and sharing with others still struggling is beautiful and powerful.

Change what you can to better yourself. Find out what works and do it. We have to develop wisdom and self-control. Three times in my life the police were involved with getting me to the hospital. Each time as I first saw them, I submitted and things went better. If you find yourself with authorities, try to find a happy place and breathe and submit. It is not worth fighting. This is harder for some of us than others.

I have a tendency to want to blame others in my life when things do not go my way. Ultimately it is me who needs to take the responsibility to make changes and live differently. No one can do it for me. You are doing it. It can take time. We have to have patience.

Find people whom you trust and build a bridge to talk, cry, laugh, or scream. It is important that we have social connections. Each of us has different social needs and it is important to realize that this can change as we live our lives. Life challenges us constantly to adapt to new changes and experiences. Just when we get into a groove, things may change and we will have to adapt.

Get to know yourself and the challenges that you face. We each have our own purpose and dreams. Do you still have dreams? I find that my dreams are intermittent at times and occasionally they disappear into the darkness. When they do come back to life, sometimes they are better than before.

Self-sabotage is one of the hardest for people to understand and eliminate. Sometimes it is deeply rooted and needs to be worked on from different angles to get to the source of the pain. Trauma can affect us to be stuck in cycles. It can be challenging to move on from the suffering.

We need to let go of beating ourselves up and instead choose to forgive ourselves and others. The self-isolation hatred cycle and self-harm can be worked through. Please continue to reach out for help. We can work through our generational trauma to not pass it on. We can pass the light of healing onward to the next generations.

Do not accept the worst case scenario for your future. Believe a better existence is around the corner. You've got this. Even if you drop the ball, you can pick it up again and you can do better next time.

I was a Safety Lead Advisor at a large facility and members of our safety team had gotten sick and I attempted to cover their duties for them. I eventually broke down and had a mild-manic-psychotic episode that resulted in going to the onsite health centre. I quickly vanished off-site with the Project Manager and we went to the town hospital. It resulted in ending my job with that company in a quiet way. It was a jarring experience to enter the hospital confines after weeks of heavy responsibilities.

My wife rescued me from the chaos of the hospital and I got better at home. Depression followed and I eventually got back in the saddle of life and safety work. I worked safety at many facilities near by that one where I got sick and it was always that same facility that was in the back of my mind as a point of fear.

It took me close to ten years to go back to that facility. I did go back and I survived it. It was strange to be in the same places that I had my episode in. It felt great to face the fear and work through it and choose life.

You can do it too. You can rise up and face your challenges. You are going for it. Your present reality does not have to remain forever. You can do it. You can get back up and go for it once again. Be strong and courageous.

Become your own advocate and build a case of what works for you, and what doesn't. Each and every one of us is unique and special. We share traits and experiences with others yet we each have different challenges to face.

Do not act on the impulses if you are having any. Practice self-control. It is vital to control impulses that potentially have negative consequences. Use the help of your support group as you transition to knowing what is a good impulse. Proactively think through your impulses to know which is worthwhile to actually take a chance on. Perhaps use index prompt cards that are pre-written to help you think and act your chosen way. Write them out with others from your support group if need be.

Any label or diagnoses does not define me or my family member. We are human beings first and foremost who need to live with love in our lives. We need to be in community and connect with someone else.

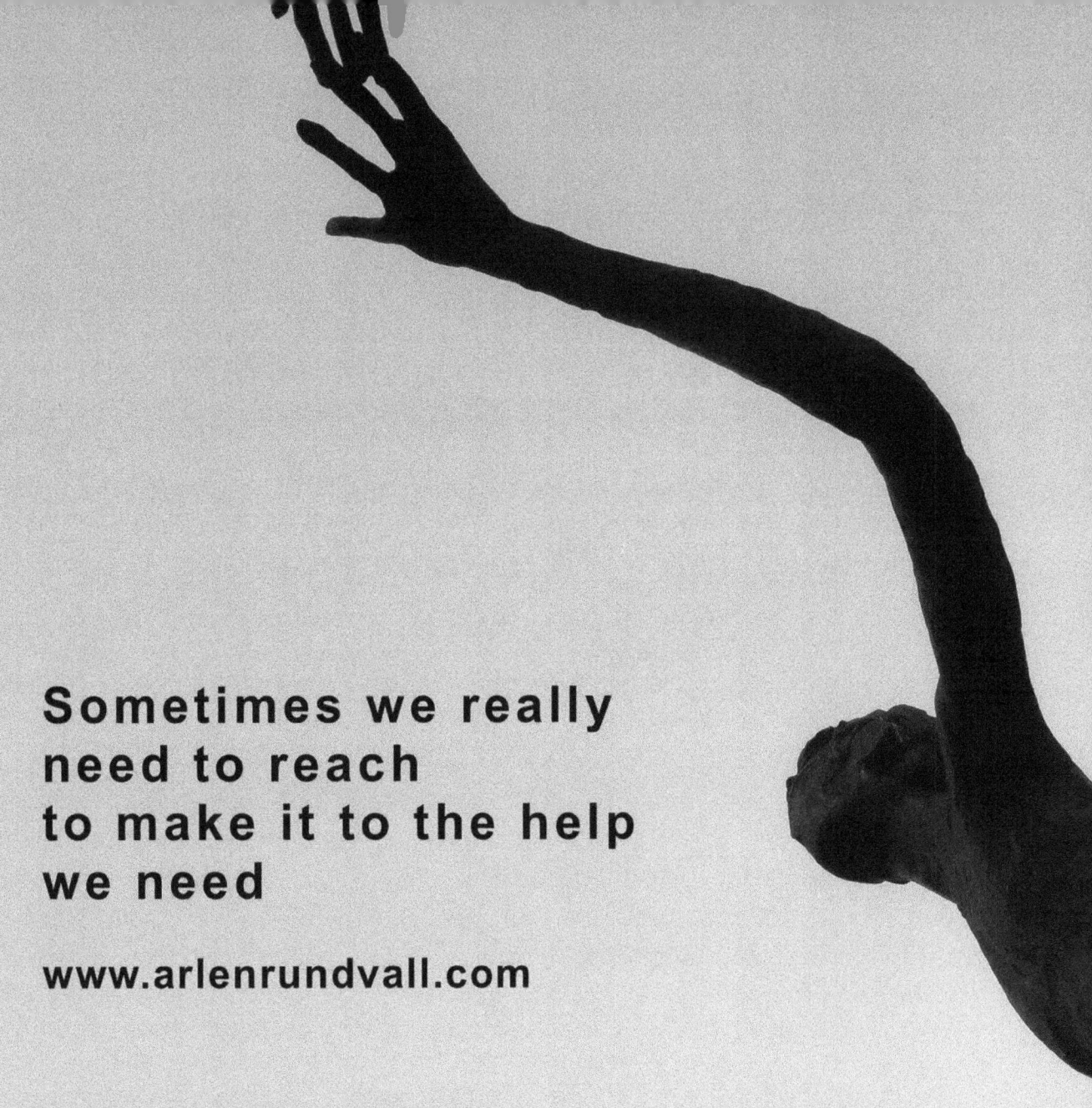

**Sometimes we really
need to reach
to make it to the help
we need**

www.arlenrundvall.com

Diagnoses can help us know what we are facing as far as challenges and to know what we are up against as far as patterns. We can study our illness challenges and learn ways to control the negatives, and work hard to break free from the negative patterns.

We all need love and acceptance on some level. Love the person as they are. Do not judge the person if the person is past self-control with illness. Do not accept the behaviour if it is damaging. We need to learn to control our behaviour and project our healthy best. We also need to learn to forgive our loved ones and ourselves.

Accept the person for being out there where they are at in their journey. Try to meet them where they are on some level. Even times of psychosis are real for the person going through it. It could be just providing a blanket for warmth or a glass of water for thirst.

At times in the midst of illness we can be incapable of rational thought. We still need to care for our basic needs and safety. We also need to ensure the safety of our loved ones and community. We may have to be protected from ourselves. Our community may have to be protected from us. Mental Illness is a complex foe.

Meeting the physical needs of nutrition and rest will help our mind. We are all intertwined with our physical-mental-emotional-spiritual health. We need to care for our whole self.

Try to do the best that you can in each moment. We can learn to care for ourselves and learn that we are worthy of self-love. Practice when to forgive yourself and when to give yourself a kick forward to get it done. Sometimes we need to change the approach and learn how to do more detailed self-care.

Do something good for yourself and your loved ones. It can be a simple pat on your own back. Celebrate your achievements. Celebrate others and what they are able to be or do. Sometimes getting out of bed and taking a shower is an achievement if we are not feeling well.

Flowers and cards of encouragement are nice to receive or give. Encourage others and you will find encouragement yourself. Ask me how I am doing and really care to listen unconditionally.

Empower me to make my own decisions to live with the consequences. Protect and love me yet let me learn on my own and flounder a bit to make my own way.

Build healthy creative outlets to deal with the pain, the bizarre, and the suffering. It is important that we acknowledge these challenges on some level. If we ignore them, they will tend to continue in their cycles. If we embrace them in some way and learn to work through them and perhaps be creative, we can liberate ourselves in small ways that can build up toward bigger cathartic breakthroughs.

Be aware of what thoughts, feelings, and actions hurt you and do not do them. It can be hard to let go if it is a pattern or an addiction. Try to taper off or go cold turkey and eliminate it. Harm reduction can be a step toward whole freedom. There are support groups out there to help with addiction. Work with your professionals. Ultimately, we have to face addiction down in our own minds and bodies. There are proven ways to help with these support programs. They teach us to work on our living problems. Easy does it.

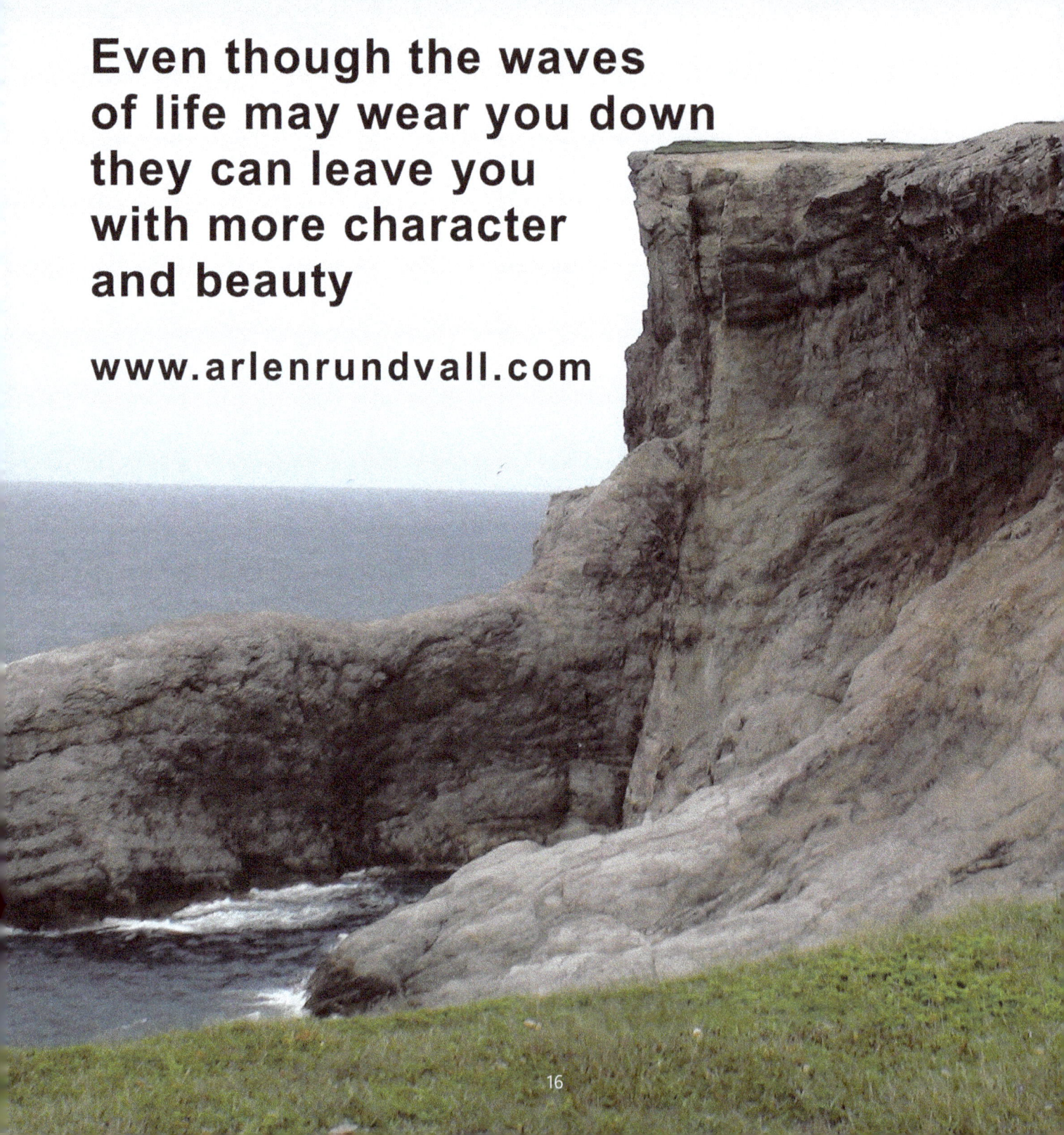

Things can always get worse and sometimes they do yet there is always something to be thankful for. Just to be alive is a gift. Sometimes we can get sidetracked and dwell on poor me. You have a choice to dwell there as long as it serves you. You can choose now to let go and let a glimmer of hope back in. Sometimes a simple smile you give someone opens your heart to receive a smile in return. You shared something of beauty. Gratitude enhances attitude. Being thankful changes our perspective and can have huge outcomes in our lives.

It is vital to become experts in cultivating hope. Build a hope chest of pictures, memories, music, and other items that will encourage you. Get help to build this if you are finding yourself too low. It is dangerous to face death down without any hope. To dwell in fear and not involve anyone else for help is dangerous. If and when we visit suicidal thinking, we need our hope and the hope of others to focus and build on.

As a family member, look after your own needs first and watch out for triggers that you may pull with each other. We can get intertwined with others and have seemingly automatic triggers and outcomes. Things play out with each other sometimes in the same ways. Learn together to avoid pushing negative buttons. Strive to develop and to push the positive buttons. It can be hard to get out of the rut of the cycles of interaction. We have to do something different to get different results. Sometimes we need to use a different level and style of thinking to solve our problem.

It can be hard not to hold a grudge and blame others for what they did to us. We need to journey through to the place to forgive them and learn how to move on. We need to learn how to forgive ourselves. These steps can be a great challenge yet are essential for us to work through to a more peaceful existence.

Our lives depend on our abilities to face the wind of challenges and to learn how to look after ourselves. It is up to us to know how we learn best. Then we need to learn what we need to learn. We have to learn how to self-treat with healthy pursuits and to reduce and eliminate self-treating with negative pursuits and substances.

Look for the best doctor that you can find and do not be afraid to look again if it is not working. Sometimes the first doctor and the first medication we take can be excellent for us and at other times it takes a few tries. Work on as many other things that you can to better your mental health so that you do not have to be on as much medication. For example, going for regular walks can help achieve this. You can work with your professionals to develop other approaches.

Just because you thought it, doesn't mean you have to act upon it or feel it.

Just because you feel it, doesn't mean you have to think it, or act on it.

Just because you acted, doesn't mean you have to think about it or feel it.

Unless you want to...

www.arlenrundvall.com

Get over it. Mental illness is in your family and your neighbourhood. Everyone experiences a form and degree of mental health. I have talked to some people who take pride in stating that they know no one with mental illness. Is this possible? Occasionally there is a smugness about it. I am certain that they interact with people who are indeed struggling with mental illness yet are able to act with excellence to cover it up.

We have to be careful with our acting, our faking it before making it. It can have great aspects in getting through situations where we may be scared to do the task or be in the situation. If we are always acting it can become a hollow-forced existence. We need to find some people we can let our guard down with and be ourselves.

We live in a demanding world. We cannot avoid mental health and illness so we need to learn to live with it in our communities, our families, our workplaces, and in ourselves.

Try to laugh again. We only have so many tears. It is a test of how seriously we are taking ourselves if we can laugh. Life can be pretty heavy sometimes. Sometimes we need a laugh to bring healing and humour into our situations.

Mental illness is a dire challenge that requires earnest responsibility to learn how to develop the user manual for our lives. No one person gives us all the answers or fixes us. We need to learn to look after ourselves with the help of our personal and professional support networks.

This is what it took to wake me up out of my many cycles of hospitalizations for manic episodes in my twenties. I waded into a spring-thawed river with chunks of ice in it. I was having a delusion of being a stunt person and got the impulse to successfully do a backflip in a river with water up to my waist. I landed on my head on the rock bottom with incredible pain in my head, neck, and shoulders. I stood up and clasped my neck in terror and fell back into the cradle of the cold river water. The current took me down the river. It was incredibly painful and hard to get out of the situation.

It gave me the wake up call that I needed to take control of my mental health. I was embracing my manic highs and enjoying parts of them a little too much. I learned the hard way that if I continued down pathways lacking control, I rolled the dice with potential painful consequences.

I learned to study my gateway experiences that drove me toward manic highs. One of them was getting excited about God and spirituality. I learned to cool down my spiritual experiences. I discovered over the years a deeper foundation of spirituality that does not cause me harm.

Even on the darkest days
Look through the rain

www.arlenrundvall.com

Be careful with your impulses. Practice not acting on the negative outcome impulses. It is vital to develop this skill. Focus on the positive. Choose life. Be empowered to exercise your choice to live with the consequences. We need to develop a proactive approach to our challenges. Work on this with your support network.

We can learn how to take care of ourselves and be well and then things may change up and we need to adapt and try a different approach. I find it to be an ever-changing sparring partner. I just get into some progress and then things change up and I have a new foe to face. Sometimes I need to adapt with the flow more than fighting my challenges head on.

Sometimes it is a great accomplishment to simply not hurt ourselves. We can be stuck in a pattern of self-harm that is difficult to get out of. You are worth it. Try it a day or an hour at a time. You can break free through learning to forgive others and yourself and getting to the root of patterns. Perhaps substitute a lesser harm to wean yourself down. You can make progress.

Your present situation does not have to be your last. It is up to you to change. You can do it. You are doing it. You are the creator of your existence. It starts with your thoughts and feelings and actions.

We are each different as far as relationship needs go. Some of us may need more alone time. Others of us are always surrounded with people. We should develop the ability to know if we need alone time or who is best to spend time with.

It is better being single than with the wrong person. Look after yourself. Heal yourself and reduce your baggage as a single person before bringing that baggage into a relationship. There is time to find the right person to be in relationship with. You will find that special person because you are becoming that special person.

Do not accept defeat. Try one more day to live. Get up again and again. The days will get brighter. Keep on keeping on. Throw on your favourite music and dance. Try to believe one positive thing.

Mental health challenges can hamper our quality of life and threaten our very existence. We do and will bounce back to better days. You are doing it. Be patient and give it time and do good things for yourself and others. Help someone else out if you can. Get out of self-obsession and your problems and help someone with their situation. The end result is most likely that both of your problems will be reduced.

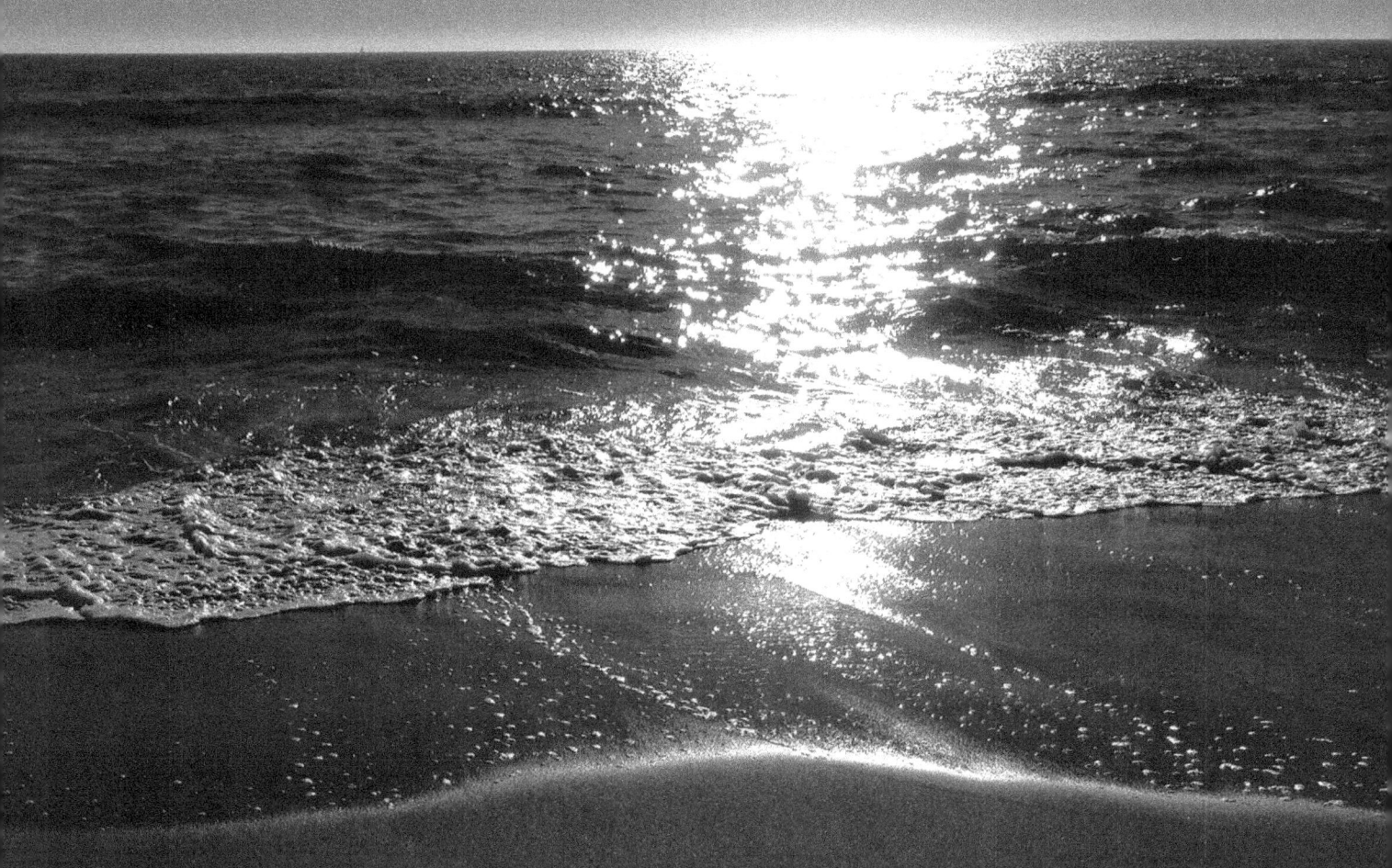

Be responsible for yourself. You can help others yet they are ultimately responsible for their own lives. Beware of getting sucked into other people's drama when it is too much for you to handle. There is a time to walk away. Sometimes the greatest love we can demonstrate is to simply avoid a person, because we do not mix well together. Not everyone can get along with everyone.

We need to be thankful for positive people in our lives and build trusting relationships. It is sometimes not easy to be with people when you are struggling. We can choose who we spend our time with and be empowered. Learn to love others. It is hard to let go of the judge and let others be. Sometimes we need to allow others to flounder. They are on their own journey. Sow seeds of hope and courage for them. If you believe in prayer, pray for them. Send good thoughts their way.

Learn to love yourself. It can be hard to feel worthy. Life can beat us down to the point of not feeling worthy of love. You deserve love and a sense of freedom from harm in your life. Please do or think something nice for yourself. Beauty begins with giving. If you can't give good thoughts for yourself, start with giving good thoughts for someone else and move toward being nice to yourself.

Many of us have done things that we regret and have caused ourselves and perhaps others pain and suffering. Some of us are stuck in generational patterns of harm. Take a small step today to lessen its effect and turn away and treat yourself better. Please don't pass it on to your children. Seek and find the grace to let go of past hurt. Don't promote it in yourself or others anymore. Stop the negative and continue with the positive. Share some light.

Learn to plant your mind-garden well and nurture it. Your mind needs cultivating and pruning and nourishment. We expect much from our minds and it is vital that we invest in them so that we can treat ourselves and others with love and kindness. Be empowered to take more control. You can do it. It takes practice.

Sea is sky sky is sea
I help you you help me

www.arlenrundvall.com

I hope that you found this book to be cathartic and freeing. I hope that it is of encouragement to you. Your life is your life to live and shine. Seek freedom. Help others. Help yourself to what you need for a better existence.

I encourage you to pursue good direction at your crossroads in life. Remember to face the rain. The sun will shine again.

I have learned to live with grief, addiction, depression, mania, psychosis, and anxiety. Throughout, there have been physical health challenges as well. Thanks to everyone who helped me on my journey. Thankfully I have learned to face adversity and work through the weather of my journey. I am not perfect and continue to learn to maintain my balance.

I have found that I have learned much from the challenges that I have faced. Very mild depression helps me to edit my writing. A bit of mania helps me to be bold and go for it. Anxiety helped me as a Safety Advisor to be there, for our workers, through hazard assessments. Grief built a bridge to others who are going through grief themselves. Addiction taught me to face down my substances of choice and to have grace. Most of all, mental illness gave me the opportunity to build compassion and empathy.

The storms come and go as I continue down the path, round the next corner, I hope to travel lighter. I choose to drop some baggage now and find good direction at the next crossroads.

Perhaps our paths will cross again and it won't be raining quite so hard.

We are on a journey and I am thankful that we met in these pages. Thank you for reading *Face the Rain*. I would encourage you to write your own *Mental Health Essentials*. We may share some things that work for each of us yet you are unique and have your own needs.

Remember that you are the creator of your existence. Your present reality can and will change with your outlook, choices, and actions.

All the best on your journey,

Arlen

Stop and Think (Strengthen my Executive Function)

I breathe in my nose slowly and breathe out my mouth slowly.
I slow down my breathing.
I involve my senses in my surroundings to ground myself.

- What am I thinking of doing?
- What are my options to keep myself safe?
- How can I guard against hurting myself or others?
- What effect does it have short term and long term?
- Can I remember past times that my decision hurt me?
- I forgive myself and learn a better way to not go into harm.
- What is the empowering end result of my decision?
- What are the consequences of my thoughts, feelings, and actions?
- I think about consequences before I act.
- I own my decision to act and the results are my responsibility.
- I think of my good actions through to good results.
- I am empowered to live my life in positive ways.

Consult with your Health Professionals   www.arlenrundvall.com

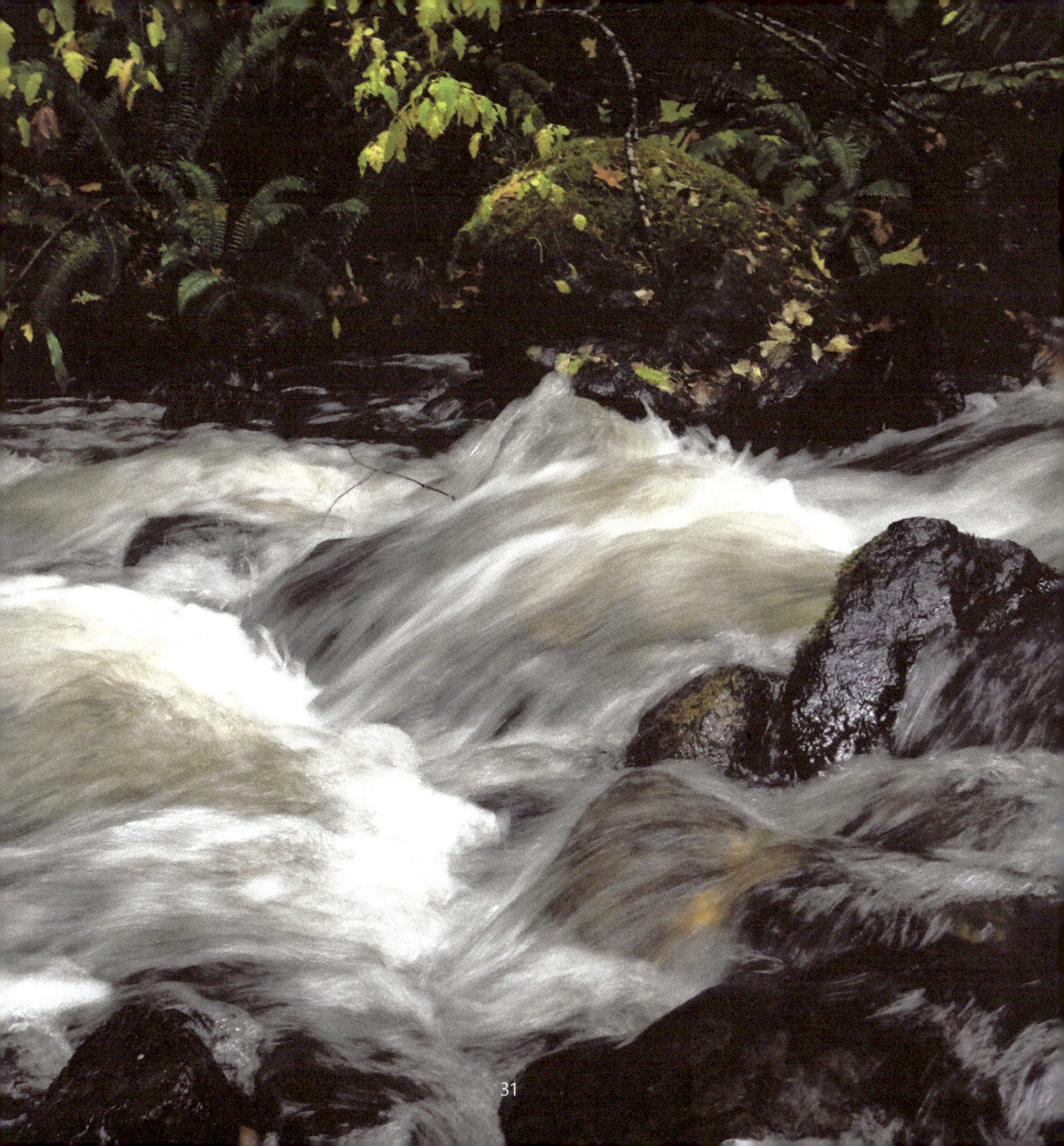

www.ingramcontent.com/pod-product-compliance
Lightning Source LLC
Chambersburg PA
CBHW040544220526
45473CB00016B/3019